WEALTHY AND WELL

Strategies For Building Wealth While Priorities Health

Dr Sebastian Wayne

CONTENTS

COVER PAGE

COPYRIGHT

TABLE OF CONTENT

INTRODUCTION

CHAPTER 1

UNDERSTANDING WEALTH

IMPORTANCE OF BALANCE

YOUR DREAM ECONOMIC AND YOUR WELL BEING

CHAPTER 2

MINDFUL MONEY MANAGEMENT

KEYS TO CONSTRUCTING WEALTH

INVEST

TYPES OF INVESTMENT

SHOULD I PAY OFF DEBT OR INVEST

WHAT IS AN EXCHANGE TRADED FUNDS (E.T.E)

BUDGETING, SAVINGS AND INVESTMENT

CHAPTER 3

CREATING PASSIVE INCOME

WAYS TO GENERATING YOUR WEALTH

WEALTH WITHOUT SACRIFICING YOUR HEALTH
AND WELL BEING

CHAPTER 4

HEALTHY HABITS FOR WEALTH BUILDERS

THINGS NOT TO GIVE TO ACQUIRED WEALTH

HEALTHY SACRIFICE FOR WEALTH

CHAPTER 5

WORK LIFE BALANCE

TECHNIQUES TO PUTTING BOUNDARIES

ACTIONS TO TAKE

RECOMMENDATIONS

Introduction

Understanding the nuanced relationship between wealth and wellness is paramount in today's society, where material prosperity often intersects with individual and societal well-being. While wealth traditionally conveys financial abundance, wellness encompasses physical, mental, and emotional health. Exploring the dynamic interplay between these two domains illuminates not only the opportunities afforded by affluence but also the complexities and challenges in achieving holistic well-being. In this introduction, we delve into the intricate tapestry of wealth and wellness, examining their intersections, impacts, and the pursuit of a balanced and fulfilling life."

CHAPTER 1

Understanding Wealth

Wealth commonly refers to an abundance of valuable resources or possessions, frequently in the form of monetary assets, property, or different tangible goods. It encompasses now not solely monetary riches however also belongings such as investments, actual estate, businesses, and precious possessions. Additionally, wealth can lengthen past fabric possessions to encompass factors such as knowledge, social connections, and private well-being, which contribute to an individual's usual prosperity and pleasant of life. Wealth is the accumulation of valuable financial sources owned via individuals, communities, companies, or countries. It encompasses all property of worth, including physical and intangible assets, minus debts. Wealth can be measured in terms of real goods or financial value, with internet worth being a frequent measure calculated through subtracting money owed from whole asset value. Unlike income, which is a float variable, wealth is a stock variable representing the valuable financial items gathered at a particular factor in time. The thinking of wealth varies amongst societies and can be expressed through a range of capability such as money, land, livestock, or different resources. Ultimately, wealth is about having monetary freedom, security, and the capability to fulfil one's desires and desires except stress or constraints.

Wealth can be similarly understood as the accumulation of belongings and sources that maintain fee and make contributions to an individual's or entity's monetary balance and prosperity. This accumulation can take quite a number forms:

1. Financial Assets: These consist of cash held in bank accounts, stocks, bonds, mutual funds, retirement accounts, and different investment vehicles. Financial belongings generate income through interest, dividends, capital gains, or different types of returns.

2. Real Estate: Ownership of land,

buildings, or other homes constitutes actual wealth. Real estate can admire over time, providing possibilities for wealth accumulation via property If you're in your prime earning years, your focus is likely on building the wealth you will need to live well in retirement. Americans are living longer and health care costs are rising. Investing enough money to provide sufficient income to sustain your current lifestyle can help pave the way for a more secure retirement. But too much focus on meeting future income needs can be stressful particularly when you are in your 30s, 40s and 50s and may be facing many family commitments. How do you find a balance? Start by realizing that it's normal to feel a nerve-wracking pull between enjoying your life today and accumulating sufficient wealth to cover all your expenses in retirement. "Thinking about how much income you will need in retirement can be very daunting," says Tracie McMillon, CFA, Head of Global Asset Allocation at Wells Fargo Investment Institute. For most people, prime working years are also prime family years — the time when children are growing up and older family members may begin to need medical care. Having a single-minded focus on wealth-building at the expense of family priorities can cause major stress, which can even impact your health. More than just an annoyance, chronic stress raises the risk of heart disease, high blood pressure, diabetes, depression, anxiety disorder, and other illnesses. Burying your head in the sand isn't the answer, either. "People tend to focus more on the present than the future," says Margie E. Lochmann, Ph.D., professor of psychology and director of the Lifespan Initiative on Healthy Aging and Lifespan Lab at Brandeis University. While it can be fun to live in the moment, the secret to building wealth without damaging your health lies in taking a balanced approach. Here are six ways to find a work-life balance that allows you to enjoy today while saving for tomorrow.

1) Don't wait

If you don't think that you will be able to meet your income needs in retirement, don't waste time beating yourself up about it. Meet with your financial team now to take immediate action. You may want to consider whether you are accumulating wealth in the most tax-efficient accounts and also revisit your regular expenditures. Having a clear plan in place can help you increase opportunities available to you when you retire.

2) Rethink retirement income

When interest rates are high, many retired investors look to bond portfolios for income. But with sustained low interest rates, those accumulating wealth for retirement as well as those already in retirement may need to consider other avenues to generate their income.

"Sometimes, fear of risk makes people too conservative with retirement savings. They don't want to lose what they've worked so hard for," McMillon says. "But you do want to get a good return on your money. Requote Because people are living longer in retirement, you may want to keep exposure to equities and other growth investments even as you get closer to retirement. A portfolio that relies solely on fixed income may not be able to keep up with inflation. "Talk to your investment specialist to determine which strategies align with your specific needs," offers McMillon.

3) Involve your family

Take advantage of opportunities to talk

with your family about finances. When your children are young, it can help to explain why it's so important for you to save for the future and that sometimes short-term sacrifices are necessary to make that happen. Understanding the family's financial realities may help lower everyone's stress levels when you occasionally have to make the choice to skip a Little League game or gymnastics meet in order to put in some extra hours at work. By having regular conversations about budgeting and investing, your children will be well informed as they mature and more prepared for their own financial futures.

4) Take care of your health

Neglecting self-care not only interferes with your quality of life but can also make your post-retirement health care costs skyrocket. Protect your health and your nest egg by eating a healthy diet, exercising most days of the week, maintaining a healthy weight, getting regular health check-ups, and staying up to date on vaccinations. These things do take time and effort, but they can have big payoffs later in life.

5) Make your money work as hard as you do

Business owners often have their company's balance sheet top of mind as they build their business. But once the business is passed along, their personal balance sheet will need to be structured to sustain them. As always, diversification and asset placement are key strategies to help plan for growth and income in a portfolio. Your investment professional can help you evaluate your current allocation against your anticipated needs and recommend adjustments to help keep you on track.

6) Think beyond dollars

Investing cash during your prime earning years is important, of course. But it's also essential to plan in a more holistic way as well. "Make investments in the future — not just monetary ones, but also in relationships, health, career, and education," Lochmann says. "They all can pay big dividends in the long run. "development.

- Business Ownership: Owning fairness in businesses or entrepreneurial ventures can be a substantial supply of wealth. Successful agencies generate profits, dividends, or capital gains for their owners.

- Intellectual Property: Patents, copyrights, trademarks, and different forms of intellectual property can symbolize precious assets, generating earnings via licensing agreements, royalties, or sales.

- Valuable Possessions: Luxury objects such as artwork, jewellery, collectibles, or high-end automobiles can make a contribution to one's typical wealth, both by conserving or appreciating in value.

- Human Capital: Knowledge, skills, expertise, and trip also make contributions to wealth. Investing in education, training, and personal improvement can decorate earning viable and career opportunities, thereby growing common wealth.

Wealth is not completely measured through the extent of assets one possesses but additionally through elements such as liquidity (the ease of converting belongings into cash), steadiness (the sustainability of wealth over time), and diversification (spreading wealth throughout quite a number assets to mitigate risks). Moreover, wealth can provide get right of entry to opportunities, privileges, and a greater preferred of living, however it does now not assurance happiness or fulfilment. Balancing wealth accumulation with different components of life, such as health, relationships, and private fulfilment, is integral for holistic well-being. Wealth differs from earnings in various key aspects. Income represents the float of money obtained regularly, such as wages, salaries, or business profits, whilst wealth signifies the accrued assets and ordinary fee of one's monetary holdings. Income is the cash or income received over a specific period, while wealth refers to the whole belongings owned, inclusive of cash, property, investments, and possessions. Income can fluctuate primarily based on factors like employment or funding returns, whilst wealth fluctuates primarily based on modifications in asset values or investments. Income is indispensable for day-to-day costs and assembly financial obligations, whilst wealth displays a person's usual monetary position and long-term security. Additionally, earnings is problem to taxation, whereas wealth is now not at once taxed but can be concern to taxes on capital good points or property. Ultimately, earnings is about the flow of money, while wealth represents the accumulated resources that provide monetary protection and possibilities for constructing generational wealth. Income plays a indispensable function in shaping wealth over time. Income, as the waft of money acquired regularly, contributes to the accumulation of wealth by way of supplying the assets wanted to collect assets and investments. Consistent income streams enable folks to save, invest, and construct their wealth over time. For example, earnings from employment, enterprise profits, or investments can be used to purchase property, stocks, or different property that respect in fee and contribute to typical wealth accumulation.

Moreover, greater incomes often lead to multiplied financial savings and investment opportunities, which can further boost wealth growth. Individuals with higher incomes have extra ability to store and invest, permitting them to construct a large economic cushion and generate extra profits thru investments. On the other hand, fluctuations in income can affect wealth accumulation. Job loss or reduced profits may hinder the capability to retailer and invest, slowing down the boom of wealth over time.

In essence, a steady and adequate earnings is critical for building wealth over time as it offers the skill to collect assets, make investments, and secure economic balance for the future.

Let's delve deeper into how income influences wealth over time:

1. Asset Acquisition:

- Income as a Tool: Income serves as a tool for obtaining assets that make a contribution to wealth accumulation. Regular profits permits persons to save and invest in belongings like real estate, stocks, or businesses, which recognize in value over time.

- Diversification: Higher income ranges grant the probability to diversify investments, reducing chance and doubtlessly growing wealth thru various asset classes.

2. Savings and Investments:

- Saving Capacity: Income degrees decide the ability to save cash for future desires or investments. Higher incomes frequently lead to larger savings, accelerating wealth growth.

- Investment Opportunities: Income permits people to discover investment possibilities that generate additional profits streams, such as dividends, interest, or capital gains.

3. Financial Stability:

- Emergency Funds: Adequate profits permits for the creation of emergency funds, safeguarding wealth from surprising prices or profits disruptions.

- Debt Management: Income influences the ability to control debts effectively, stopping activity expenses from eroding wealth over time.

4. Long-Term Planning:

- Retirement Planning: Income plays a vital position in retirement planning by using deciding the quantity people can retailer for retirement and preserve their lifestyle post-retirement.

- Generational Wealth: Higher incomes facilitate the introduction of generational wealth by passing down assets and economic expertise to future generations.

5. Impact of Income Fluctuations:

- Risk Mitigation: Fluctuations in income can have an effect on wealth accumulation by means of affecting savings and funding capacity. Planning for profits variability is vital to mitigate dangers to wealth growth.

- Adaptability: Individuals with the potential to adapt to profits fluctuations via budgeting, saving in the course of high-income periods, and diversifying income sources can higher maintain wealth increase over time.

Profits is a indispensable driver of wealth accumulation, supplying the potential to acquire assets, save, invest, and impenetrable monetary steadiness for the future. Strategic administration of income, along with prudent financial planning, is necessary for sustained wealth increase over time.

Health is the largest wealth for a human being in his/her entire lifetime. One can live on without excess cash but can't live on besides correct health. Health is some thing that we can't buy with money however we can take care of it and we can therapy it when needed with the assist of the money. If a character is now not having precise health, he will now not be in a position to experience his/her lifestyles to the fullest. Money doesn't make a character rich and blissful but suitable health does. Moreover, a person can't experience whole and completely happy except exact health. Good fitness is one of the foremost factors of happiness that a individual wants in his/her life. We can see a number of human beings around us that are completely happy except having a lot of money. However, they are glad due to the fact they have desirable fitness and they enjoy their lives. We can also see many human beings that are having a lot of cash and are rich ample to purchase anything they favour however still, they are not completely happy. Moreover, they are no longer relaxed with their lives. The reason in the back of the sadness of the rich human beings is frequently that they don't have top health and they worry about this element a lot. However, they can't buy excellent fitness with their money.

Importance Of Balance

Balancing wealth and fitness is integral for average well-being. Financial stability gives peace of mind, reduces stress, and helps relationships. Good health is integral for every day activities, work performance, and enjoying life's pleasures.

Neglecting health can lead to untimely getting older and prevent success. Striving for balance in fitness and wealth is key to a pleasant life, as they are interconnected and have an impact on each other. Achieving equilibrium in these areas involves self-commitment, accountability, and intentional effort. Imbalance can lead to struggles, unhappiness, and barriers in life. Recognizing the significance of balance, looking for professional advice, and making personal boom adjustments are imperative steps closer to a extra fulfilling and contented life. Remember, a harmonious mixture of health, wealth, and happiness is essential for a well-rounded and pleasurable life. If you're in your prime earning years, your focus is likely on building the wealth you will need to live well in retirement. Americans are living longer and health care costs are rising. Investing enough money to provide sufficient income to sustain your current lifestyle can help pave the way for a more secure retirement. But too much focus on meeting future income needs can be stressful particularly when you are in your 30s, 40s and 50s and may be facing many family commitments. How do you find a balance? Start by realizing that it's normal to feel a nerve-wracking pull between enjoying your life today and accumulating sufficient wealth to cover all your expenses in retirement. "Thinking about how much income you will need in retirement can be very daunting," says

Tracie McMillon, CFA, Head of Global Asset Allocation at Wells Fargo Investment Institute. For most people, prime working years are also prime family years

— the time when children are growing up and older family members may begin to need medical care. Having a single-minded focus on wealth-building at the expense of family priorities can cause major stress, which can even impact your health. More than just an annoyance, chronic stress raises the risk of heart disease, high blood pressure, diabetes, depression, anxiety disorder, and other illnesses. Burying your head in the sand isn't the answer, either. "People tend to focus more on the present than the future," says Margie E. Lochmann, Ph.D., professor of psychology and director of the Lifespan Initiative on Healthy Aging and Lifespan Lab at Brandeis University. While it can be fun to live in the moment, the secret to building wealth without damaging your health lies in taking a balanced approach. Here are six ways to find a work-life balance that allows you to enjoy today while saving for tomorrow.

1) Don't wait

If you don't think that you will be able to meet your income needs in retirement, don't waste time beating yourself up about it. Meet with your financial team now to take immediate action. You may want to consider whether you are accumulating wealth in the most tax-efficient accounts and also revisit your regular expenditures. Having a clear plan in place can help you increase opportunities available to you when you retire.

2) Rethink retirement income

When interest rates are high, many retired investors look to bond portfolios for income. But with sustained low interest rates, those accumulating wealth for retirement as well as those already in retirement may need to consider other avenues to generate their income.

"Sometimes, fear of risk makes people too conservative with retirement savings.

They don't want to lose what they've worked so hard for," McMillian says. "But you do want to get a good return on your money. Requote Because people are living longer in retirement, you may want to keep exposure to equities and other growth investments even as you get closer to retirement. A portfolio that relies solely on fixed income may not be able to keep up with inflation. "Talk to your investment specialist to determine which strategies align with your specific needs," offers McMillon.

3) Involve your family

Take advantage of opportunities to talk with your family about finances. When your children are young, it can help to explain why it's so important for you to save for the future and that sometimes short-term sacrifices are necessary to make that happen. Understanding the family's financial realities may help lower everyone's stress levels when you occasionally have to make the choice to skip a Little League game or gymnastics meet in order to put in some extra hours at work. By having regular conversations about budgeting and investing, your children will be well informed as they mature and more prepared for their own financial futures.

4) Take care of your health

Neglecting self-care not only interferes with your quality of life but can also make your post-retirement health care costs skyrocket. Protect your health and your nest egg by eating a healthy diet, exercising most days of the week, maintaining a healthy weight, getting regular health check-ups, and staying up to date on vaccinations. These things do take time and effort, but they can have big payoffs later in life.

5) Make your money work as hard as you do Business owners often have their

company's balance sheet top of mind as they build their business. But once the business is passed along, their personal balance sheet will need to be structured to sustain them. As always, diversification and asset placement are key strategies to help plan for growth and income in a portfolio. Your investment professional can help you evaluate your current allocation against your anticipated needs and recommend adjustments to help keep you on track.

6) Think beyond dollars Investing cash during your prime earning years is important, of course. But it's also essential to plan in a more holistic way as well. "Make investments in the future — not

just monetary ones, but also in relationships, health, career, and education," Lochmann says. "They all can pay big dividends in the long run." To attain a balance between fitness and wealth, think about sensible techniques from a range of sources:

- Set Realistic Goals: Begin via placing potential dreams that encompass both health and wealth.

- Use Fitness Trackers: Incorporate fitness trackers to screen physical pastime and doubtlessly minimize health-related costs.

- Reduce Car Usage: Opt for taking walks or biking alternatively of using to save money, improve health, and reduce environmental impact.

- Prioritize Sleep: Utilize apps that aid in attaining higher sleep quality, which is critical for typical health and performance.

- Cook at Home: Save cash and control your diet by making ready self-made meals, promotion better health and monetary management.

- Involve Family: Discuss monetary matters with your family to decrease stress and make sure each person is familiar with the importance of saving for the future.

- Self-Care: Prioritize self-care via wholesome habits like exercise, normal check-ups, and keeping a balanced weight loss plan to safeguard your health and finances.

- Invest Wisely: Diversify investments to impervious financial balance while thinking about long-term increase and earnings needs.

- Seek Professional Advice: Consult with specialists to gain know-how and self assurance in managing both health and wealth effectively.

By imposing these steps, you can work towards a harmonious balance between your fitness and wealth, leading to a extra gratifying and affluent life.

Your Dream Economic And Your Well Being

The thinking of the Dream Economy revolves round people like Elon Musk, who embody visionary ideas that captivate the public and pressure financial growth. In this context, the Dream Economy emphasizes the energy of daring predictions and myth-making to encourage self assurance and mobilize resources in the direction of formidable goals, such as Musk's imaginative and prescient of colonizing Mars. This monetary paradigm values the potential to embody hopes and fears about the future greater than just offering rational proof for a vision's feasibility. The Dream Economy intertwines with the broader financial landscape, influencing industries, public perception, and funding decisions. It highlights the importance of narratives, myths, and charismatic figures in shaping economic trajectories and fostering innovation and progress. Ultimately, the Dream Economy underscores how dreams, aspirations, and visionary leadership can power economic activities, have an impact on markets, and shape societal values and expectation.

CHAPTER 2

Mindful Money Management

Money administration entails budgeting, saving, investing, and overseeing the utilization of capital for folks or groups. It consists of growing a price range to music profits and expenses, constructing an emergency fund for sudden expenses, paying payments on time to avoid late costs and enhance credit scores, and slicing back on unnecessary recurring fees like subscriptions. Additionally, saving up cash for big purchases alternatively of relying on loans can limit activity costs. Starting an investment strategy, even with small contributions, can help generate greater profits over time. Effective cash administration is vital for attaining economic goals and improving economic well-being. Money management refers to the technique of monitoring and planning an person or group's use of capital. In private and corporate finance, money administration commonly consists of budgeting, spending, saving, and investing. Private banking financial advisors furnish money administration offerings to person customers.

Commercial banking offers money administration to company clients. In economic markets, cash management additionally refers to portfolio management and investment management. Financial experts manipulate investments and make investment decisions for pools of funds. Money management is a extensive concept. It refers to the techniques and methods to decide the use of an individual, company, or institution's capital. In private finance, money management covers budgeting, spending, and saving (investing). Money management can be proactive with periodic or ordinary monetary planning. It can also be reactive to unique occasions barring intuitive planning in advance.

As a end result of distinct ages, lifestyles, family structures, and many other factors, financial plans for individuals are different. However, the quintessential ideas of budgeting can be normally shared. For example, one easy technique of private budgeting is the "50-20-30 Budget Rule." The 50-20-30 Budget Rule suggests an man or woman spends 50% of their after-tax profits on fundamental expenditures. The necessities include residence mortgages or rents, transportation, groceries, utilities, and so on. 30% of their income have to be spent on the things that the person wants. It can include charges on partying with friends, film tickets, and vacations. The last 20% ought to be saved or invested for future economic goals. Money administration with intuitive planning and budgeting helps to reduce inessential expenditures. Such fees do not add value to an individual's living standards. They can be saved or invested for better use in the future. Money management additionally lowers the hazard of going for walks out of money. It helps humans to gain their economic desires in the long term. Money administration with intuitive planning and budgeting helps to reduce inessential expenditures. Such expenditures do now not add cost to an individual's dwelling standards. They can be saved or invested for better use in the future. Money administration additionally lowers the hazard of running out of money. It helps people to achieve their economic goals in the long term. Financial advisors in non-public banks, insurance plan firms, and other financial institutes furnish non-public cash management services. Individuals can also procedure their cash administration needs through private finance applications. Similar to private finance, cash management for company finance also includes planning and budgeting. However, the process of budgeting is quite different. A company's budgeting is basically formed via its enterprise strategies. It is built upon the company's historical economic statements and adjusted with forecasting estimates. In addition to the use of capital, company cash management additionally considers the elevating of capital – how a great deal to finance and how to finance should be determined. Money administration for corporate finance is greater complex than for individuals. Companies want professional groups to provide financial evaluation and planning. In monetary markets, cash administration additionally refers to investment management or portfolio management. Investment corporations manipulate a pool of capital from their character and institutional clients. Money managers make investments the capital in extraordinary asset instructions to generate returns. The assets include stocks, bonds, non-public equities, real estate, commodities, and so on. The companies also offer brokerage, mutual funds, ETFs, funding advice, retirement services, economic planning, and many other cash administration services. Some of the world's top money administration firms consist of The Vanguard Group, BlackRock Inc., and Fidelity Investments. Vanguard is the world's largest mutual fund company and second-largest ETF provider. BlackRock's ETF division is the largest ETF provider in the world. Its shares unit lists $1.9 trillion belongings under management. Different funding strategies are utilized relying on many factors. The factors consist of investment philosophy, purchaser threat preferences, the dimension of the fund, and many others. For example, Bridgewater Associates, as a hedge fund firm, applies a global macro investing strategy. It seeks investment possibilities from financial trends. On the other hand, The Blackstone Group, the world's largest choice funding firm, invests a lot in personal fairness and commercial actual estate. Stock portfolio management can both be passive or active. Passive portfolios make investments in ETFs and mutual cash to observe positive indices. Active portfolios are managed by management groups with particular strategies. The management of a debt portfolio typically considers savings risk, pastime price risk, and reinvestment risk. Alternative investments can similarly diversify a portfolio and lower the systematic risk. Examples of alternative investments consist of non-public equities, challenge capitals, commodities, and real estate. Portfolio and investment administration can be very complicated and requires expertise. Professional money managers apply exclusive techniques successfully to attain a greater predicted return at the given stage of risk.

Keys To Constructing Wealth

Building wealth is a intention that many people aspire to, but it can regularly seem like an overwhelming task. It takes time, effort, and discipline to be successful with this goal, so don't be lured by means of get-rich-quick schemes and too-good-to-be-true possibilities that can ship you down a risky path. The proper news is that there are principles and techniques that can assist absolutely everyone construct and preserve wealth over the long term. And, the until now you start inserting these into practice, the higher your possibilities of success. Below, we have outlined a number of key principles for constructing wealth, including placing dreams and developing a plan, investing in schooling and skills, managing debt, saving and investing, defending your assets, perception the have an impact on of taxes, and constructing a strong credit score history. In this article, we will take a nearer seem to be at every of these concepts and how they can assist you attain your economic goals. Earn Money.

1. The first issue you want to do is start making money. This step may seem elementary however is the most fundamental one for these who are simply starting out. You've possibly considered charts displaying that a small amount of cash generally saved and allowed to compound over time in the end can grow

into a good sized sum. But these charts never answer this fundamental question: How do you get money to store in the first place? There are two basic methods of making money: through earned income or passive income. Earned income comes from what you do for a living, whilst passive earnings is derived from investments. You may additionally no longer have any passive profits until you've earned ample money to start investing. If you are either about to start a profession or taking into consideration a career change, these questions may additionally assist you figure out on what you choose to do—and the place your earned earnings is going to come from.

2. Set Goals and Develop a Plan

What will you use your wealth for? Do you prefer to fund your retirement—maybe even an early retirement? Pay for your youngsters to go to college? Buy a second home? Donate your wealth to charity? Setting goals is an quintessential first step in building wealth. When you have a clear vision of what you prefer to achieve, you can create a plan that will assist you get there. Start by way of defining your economic goals, such as saving for retirement, buying a home, or paying off debt. Be particular about the quantity of money you need to achieve each aim and the time body in which you hope to achieve it. Once you have set your goals, you need to develop a graph for accomplishing them. This can also contain growing a price range to assist you store extra money, growing your earnings via education or profession advancement, or investing in property that will admire in fee over time. Your graph should be realistic, flexible, and cantered on the lengthy term. Regularly overview your progress, and make adjustments as wanted to maintain your self on track.

3. Save Money

Simply making cash won't help you construct wealth if you end up spending it all. Moreover, if you don't have enough money saved up for your near-term obligations (like bills, rent, or mortgage) or for an emergency, then you prioritize saving sufficient above all else. Many specialists recommend having countless months' (e.g., three to six) really worth of earnings saved up for such situations. To set greater money apart for building wealth, consider these moves:

Track your spending for at least a month. You would possibly want to use a monetary software program package deal to assist you do this, however a small, pocket-size pocket book may want to also suffice. Record your every expenditure, no rely how small; many people are amazed to see where all their cash goes.

Find the fats and trim it. Break down your expenses into needs and wants. Food, shelter, and apparel are obvious needs. Add health insurance plan premiums to that list, along with auto insurance if you personal a car and life insurance plan if different people are based on your income. Many other charges will in basic terms be wants. Set a financial savings goal. Once you have a real looking thought of how a great deal cash you can set aside every month, attempt to stick to it. This doesn't imply that you have to live like a miser or be frugal all the time. If you're assembly your financial savings goals, sense free to reward your self and splurge (an splendid amount) as soon as in a while. You'll sense better and be prompted to continue to be on course. Put saving on automatic One easy way to shop a set quantity every month is to prepare with your employer or bank to mechanically transfer a sure element of every pay check into a separate financial savings or funding account. Similarly, you can shop for retirement via having money automatically withdrawn from your pay and put into your employer's 401(k) or similar plan. Financial planners normally advocate contributing at least sufficient to get your employer's full matching contribution. Find high-yield savings. Maximize the payoff of your financial savings via shopping for the savings debts that have the perfect hobby prices and lowest fees. Certificates of credit score (CDs) can be a appropriate financial savings choice if you can manage to pay for to lock up that money for a number of months or years. Keep this in mind, too: You can only reduce so tons in costs. If your expenses are already down to the bone, then you must look into ways to amplify your income.

Invest

Once you've managed to set aside some money, the subsequent step is investing it so that it will grow. Money put in financial savings is important, however the pastime fees credited on savings accounts have a tendency to be very low, and your money dangers dropping purchasing electricity over time to inflation. Perhaps the most essential investing idea for beginners (or any investor, for that matter) is diversification. Simply put, your intention have to be to spread your money among extraordinary sorts of investments. That's because investments operate otherwise at different times. For example, if the stock market is on a dropping streak, bonds may also be providing right returns. Or if Stock A is in a slump, Stock B can also be on a tear. Mutual funds supply some built-in diversification due to the fact they invest in many extraordinary securities. And you'll obtain higher diversification if you invest in each a inventory fund and a bond fund (or quite a few inventory funds and countless bond funds), for example, rather than in simply one or the other.

As every other time-honoured rule, the youthful you are, the greater danger you can have enough money to take, because you'll have extra years to make up for any losses.

Types of Investments

Investments fluctuate in phrases of danger and doable return. As a normal rule, the safer they are, the decrease their potential return, and vice versa.

If you aren't already familiar with the various types of investments, it's well worth spending a little time studying up on them. While there are all kinds of uncommon investments, most human beings will want to start with the basics: stocks, bonds, and mutual funds.

- Stocks are shares of ownership in a corporation. When you buy stock, you personal a tiny slice of that organization and will gain from any upward jostle in its share price, as nicely as any dividends that it pays out. Stocks are commonly viewed as riskier than bonds, but shares can additionally differ widely in risk from one organization to another.

- Bonds are like IOUs from a corporation or government. When you purchase a bond, the company promises to pay your money back, with interest, after a certain period. As a very standard rule, bonds are viewed much less unstable than stocks, however with less conceivable upside. At the same time, some bonds are riskier than others; bond-rating agencies assign them letter grades to reflect that.

- Mutual money are swimming pools of securities.

—often stocks, bonds, or a mixture of the two. When you purchase mutual fund shares, you get a slice of the entire pool. Mutual cash also vary in risk, depending on what they invest in.

- Protect Your Assets

You've worked hard to earn your cash and grow your wealth. The worst thing ought to be to lose it all due to a surprising tragedy or unexpected event. A furnace can burn down your house, a car accident can motive harm and clinical bills, or a premature death can suggest a loss of future income.

Insurance is a key piece of constructing your wealth due to the fact it offers protection from these and different hazards. Home insurance will change your home and property in case of a fire, auto insurance plan will make you complete after a auto accident, and life insurance will pay your beneficiaries a demise gain in the case of an untimely death. Long-term disability insurance is another type of policy that will exchange your profits if you grow to be injured, ill, or in any other case incapacitated and unable to continue working. Even young, healthy humans need to consider insurance merchandise on the grounds that they tend to end up extra steeply-priced as you grow older. That ability even if you are 25 years ancient and single, buying existence insurance then should be a lot greater comparatively cheap than when you are 10 years older with a partner, children, and mortgage.

6. Minimize the Impact of Taxes

Taxes are an often-overlooked drag on your wealth-building efforts. Of course, we are all subject to profits tax and income tax as we earn and spend money, but our investments and belongings can also be taxed. That's why it is necessary to understand your tax exposures and advance strategies to decrease their impact.

One easy way to reduce your tax invoice is to invest in tax-advantaged accounts. These accounts, such as 529 university savings plans, individual retirement bills (IRAs), and 401(k) plans, offer tax benefits that can help you shop greater cash and reduce your tax bill. For example, contributions to a typical IRA or 401(k) are tax deductible, that means that you can minimize your taxable profits and shop cash on taxes in the 12 months when you make the contribution. Moreover, they develop tax deferred, which means that when you retire and are extra possibly to be in a decrease tax bracket, the impact will be smaller. Investment positive aspects in a Roth IRA or Roth 401(k) are tax exempt, which means that you can grow and withdraw money in a Roth account besides paying taxes on any of the profits or gains.

Another strategy for minimizing taxes is to be aware of the timing and location of your investments. By preserving investments for greater than a year, you can take gain of the lower long-term capital beneficial properties tax rate, which is generally lower than the temporary capital features tax and profits tax rates. You have to additionally be conscious of the place certain belongings are held. Given the choice, an income-producing asset like a dividend-paying inventory or corporate bond should be placed in a tax-advantaged account like a

Roth IRA, where these payments will not set off taxable events. A increase inventory that will only produce capital gains (rather than income) may alternatively be better positioned in a taxable account. Manage Debt and Build Your Credit. As you build wealth, you'll begin to find it profitable to take on debt to fund a number of purchases or investments. You may also pay for things with a credit card to earn points or rewards. You may follow for a personal loan for a home or second home, a home fairness mortgage for home improvements, or an auto mortgage to buy a car. Maybe you'll want to take out a private loan to assist start a business or make investments in any individual else's.

However, it's necessary to manipulate your debt carefully—taking on too plenty debt could hinder your growth towards your wealth-building goals. To manipulate debt, be aware of your debt-to-income (DTI) ratio and make sure that your debt repayments are manageable within your budget. You need to additionally purpose to pay off high-interest debt, such as credit score card debt, as rapidly as feasible to avoid paying excessive activity charges. Be cautious of variable or adjustable pastime price products like adjustable-rate mortgages (ARMs), or these with balloon payments, as changes to the financial system or your private instances can shortly purpose these money owed to emerge as unmanageable. Indeed, if you fall into debt, your credit rating can be negatively impacted, and if you default on your debts, you should face personal bankruptcy. Maintaining a Good Credit Score

Building and retaining a correct credit score is an vital part of growing and retaining your wealth over the long term. You'll experience a lower pastime rate and higher phrases on your loans if you have a sturdy credit records and excessive credit score, which can store you heaps of bucks in hobby fees over time. Here are a few key steps that you can take to preserve a desirable credit score:

Pay your bills on time. One of the most essential factors that impacts your deposit score is your charge history. To keep a exact credit score, you must make positive to pay your payments on time, each and every time. Late payments, even if they're solely a few days late, can have a considerable negative have an effect on your credit score. Keep your credit utilization low. Your credit utilization, or the quantity of credit score you're the usage of in contrast to the quantity you have available, is another important component that influences your deposit score. To keep a appropriate deposit score, you must aim to preserve your credit score utilization under 30% of your handy credit. Avoid opening too many new accounts. Every time you follow for credit, it can have a small negative affect on your credit score. To hold a accurate credit score, you must avoid opening too many new accounts in a short length of time. Note, however, that if you do not use credit score playing cards or don't have ample deposit strains open, you may additionally fall victim to no longer having a ample credit score history. So, open some deposit playing cards and take out some loans, but do now not overdo it. By following these steps and training properly deposit habits, you can hold a appropriate savings score and maximize your borrowing power over the lengthy term.

Should I pay off debt or invest?

If you have high-interest debt, such as

many deposit card charges, it generally makes sense to pay it off earlier than you invest. Few investments ever pay as tons as credit score playing cards charge. Once you've paid off your debt, redirect that greater cash to savings and investments. And try to pay your deposit card stability in full each month, on every occasion possible, to keep away from owing interest in the future.

How a lot cash do I need to purchase a mutual fund?

Mutual fund businesses have specific minimum initial investment necessities to get started, frequently opening at about $500. After that, you can normally invest less. Some mutual money will waive their preliminary minimums if you commit to investing a everyday sum every month. You can additionally purchase mutual fund and exchange-traded fund (ETF) shares through a brokerage firm, some of which charge nothing for opening an account.

What is an exchange-traded fund (ETF)?

Exchange-traded money (ETFs) are funding swimming pools an awful lot like mutual funds. A key distinction is that their shares are traded on inventory exchanges (rather than bought and offered through a specific fund company). They once in a while charge lower charges as well. You can additionally purchase them, alongside with stocks and bonds, via a brokerage firm. While get-rich-quick schemes every so often might also be enticing, the tried-and-true way to construct wealth is thru ordinary saving and investing—and patiently permitting that cash to grow over time. It's first-class to start small. The vital factor is to start, and to begin early. Earn money and then save and make investments it smartly. Protect your belongings with insurance, and reduce your tax exposure. Remember, constructing wealth is a journey, now not a destination. Celebrate your successes alongside the way, and don't get discouraged by means of setbacks or obstacles. With patience, discipline, and a clear imaginative and prescient of your goals, you can reap monetary success and build wealth over the long term.

Budgeting, Savings And Investment

Budgeting includes growing a design to control earnings and expenses, permitting people to tune their monetary activities and make knowledgeable decisions. Savings refer to the money left after expenses, vital for emergencies and long-term economic security. Investments involve placing money into assets to generate profits or earnings over time, helping in attaining long-term financial goals like retirement or education. The 50/30/20 rule suggests allocating 50% to needs (e.g., rent, healthcare), 30% to wants (e.g., entertainment), and 20% to savings and debt (e.g., retirement). Effective budgeting, saving, and investing are crucial for financial stability, purpose achievement, and decreasing economic stress. Balancing these elements is key to monetary well-being, with ordinary monitoring and adjustments crucial for long-term success. Budgeting is the manner of growing a graph to manipulate your income and expenses. It entails monitoring your spending, placing economic goals, and allocating cash therefore to meet those goals. Saving refers to setting apart a element of your profits for future use, commonly for emergencies or particular monetary goals. It's a way to construct a economic cushion and put together for unexpected charges or long-term objectives. Investment entails placing your cash into property with the expectation of producing returns or increasing its cost over time. This could include stocks, bonds, real estate, mutual funds, or different economic instruments. Investments carry varying ranges of chance and workable for reward, depending on elements like market conditions and asset allocation.

CHAPTER 3

Creating Passive Income

Creating passive income includes generating salary with minimal ongoing effort or involvement. This can be accomplished through a number of techniques like investing in dividend-paying stocks, bonds, or rob-advisor portfolios. Owning condominium properties, starting a print-on-demand shop, self-publishing, and making monetary investments are additionally positive ways to create passive income. dandifying a area of interest market the place you can follow your expertise is vital in building passive profits streams. Passive income is earned from ventures like apartment houses or restricted partnerships the place one is no longer actively worried in every day operations . By diversifying income sources and investing wisely, people can establish streams of passive income that provide economic balance and growth over time. Creating passive profits entails producing salary with minimal ongoing effort or involvement. This can be performed through a number of techniques like investing in dividend-paying stocks, bonds, or rob-advisor portfolios. Owning condominium properties, beginning a print-on-demand shop, self-publishing, and making financial investments are additionally fine approaches to create passive income. Identifying a area of interest market where you can practice your knowledge is critical in building passive income streams. Passive earnings is earned from ventures like condominium houses or restricted partnerships the place one is not actively concerned in every day operations. By diversifying income sources and investing wisely, folks can establish streams of passive profits that supply financial steadiness and growth over time.

Ways To Generating Your Wealth

To generate wealth effectively, reflect on

consideration on investing a share of your earnings annually, as recommended via financial expert Remit Seethe. Automating savings, revisiting savings plans yearly, increasing financial savings rates, warding off high fees, and discovering energetic and passive profits sources are key steps to building wealth. Setting clear economic goals, saving consistently, investing wisely, protecting assets, minimizing tax impact, managing debt, and growing a financial graph are vital principles for wealth accumulation. Personal improvement and establishing millionaire habits are vital for humans aiming to construct wealth from humble beginnings. By following these strategies, humans can create a solid basis for wealth technology and financial security.

Some frequent errors to avoid when building wealth include:

- Not having a spending plan and budget in place.

- Putting off high-interest debt payments.

- Investing except a suitable perception of the investments.

- Living except insurance plan insurance for protection.

- Not having an emergency fund for unexpected expenses.

- Ignoring the electricity of compound

hobby in wealth accumulation.

- Not investing in the right belongings and failing to diversify investments.

- Depending solely on one earnings supply besides diversification.

- Comparing monetary development to others, main to useless pressure.

- Investing in trends besides a strong investment approach or goals.

By avoiding these mistakes and following sound monetary practices, folks can decorate their wealth-building efforts and achieve long-term economic success.

Wealth Without Sacrificing Your Health And Well Being

Wealth besides sacrificing your health and well-being is a cutting-edge thinking that emphasizes the significance of holistic achievement and attaining success besides compromising private health. Research shows a shift towards defining wealth primarily based on well-being alternatively than simply financial assets. Success is now seen as a harmonious fusion of non-public fulfilment and expert achievement, rejecting the idea of overwork and embracing sustainable growth. Prioritizing well-being over work is imperative for entrepreneurial success, highlighting the necessity of safeguarding physical, mental, and social health. It's essential to redefine success on private terms, focusing on values-driven increase and a balanced way of life that consists of time for family, hobbies, and self-care. Ultimately, the key lies in integrating work and life, making aware decisions to align professional desires with personal well-being to acquire a enjoyable and profitable life.

CHAPTER 4

Healthy Habits For Wealth Builders

Healthy habits for wealth builders embody a vary of practices that promote both financial success and normal well-being. Successful wealth builders prioritize putting unique economic goals, dwelling under their means, investing wisely, continually learning, having staying power and persistence, and understanding probability cost. These habits contain creating a clear roadmap for financial objectives, keeping disciplined spending habits, making informed funding decisions, staying up to date on economic trends, persisting through challenges, and recognizing the fee of assets like time and energy. By integrating these wholesome habits into their routines, wealth builders can obtain sustainable increase while safeguarding their physical, mental, and emotional health. Balancing financial aspirations with non-public well-being is key to long-term success in wealth building. Some tax-saving strategies for wealth builders consist of decreasing taxable income, decreasing tax rates, controlling when taxes are paid, claiming accessible tax credits, and making use of tax-efficient investment automobiles like retirement money owed and existence insurance plan policies. Wealth builders can additionally consider moving assets into tax-advantaged accounts, contributing to pre-tax savings plans, utilising usual and Roth IRAs, leveraging family planning strategies, investing in college financial savings plans, and diversifying their portfolios across extraordinary asset lessons to optimize tax efficiency and maximize wealth growth. Additionally, putting precise financial goals, dwelling below one's means, investing wisely, consistently studying about tax laws, and having endurance and persistence are quintessential habits that can make a contribution to long-term tax financial savings and wealth accumulation. By combining these techniques and habits, wealth builders can correctly control their taxes, develop their assets, and impenetrable their economic future.

Things Not To Give To Acquired Wealth

Things no longer to supply to obtained wealth encompass sacrificing family, self-esteem, and happiness for economic gain, obsessively focusing on making cash at the cost of non-public fulfilment, the usage of credit score for useless expenses, and relying on fabric possessions for confidence. Additionally, it's critical not to lose sight of the fee of time, health, proper friendship, manners, and stability in existence while pursuing wealth. Successful wealth builders understand the significance of keeping a holistic approach to wealth that encompasses monetary success barring compromising non-public well-being, relationships, and values. By warding off these pitfalls and prioritizing a balanced strategy to wealth accumulation, men and women can reap sustainable prosperity while safeguarding their universal well-being and happiness. Some frequent errors people make when trying to gather wealth encompass now not having a planned budget, ignoring the strength of compound interest, ready until they make greater cash to begin investing, attempting to time the market, failing to diversify their investments, keeping on to losing investments, and listening to standard monetary recommendation except considering person circumstances. Additionally, human beings frequently neglect the significance of having an emergency fund, dwelling barring

insurance coverage, hurrying to buy real property without assessing their financial standing, and not having a backup layout in case of income loss or emergencies. By avoiding these mistakes and adopting sound monetary practices like budgeting, investing wisely, diversifying portfolios, and preparing for unexpected circumstances, folks can enhance their wealth-building efforts and reap long-term financial security.

Healthy Sacrifice For Wealth

The thinking of wholesome sacrifice for wealth emphasizes the importance of making strategic sacrifices to obtain financial success whilst keeping standard well-being. It includes prioritizing movements that make a contribution to both wealth accumulation and non-public health. By cultivating healthy habits, such as maintaining a balanced lifestyle, nurturing relationships mindfully, and sacrificing unhealthy behaviour's like procrastination and negative eating habits, people can maintain their bodily and intellectual well-being while pursuing success. This strategy entails defining priorities, setting clear goals, embracing a boom mindset, managing time effectively, keeping financial discipline, and making informed sacrifices that align with long-term objectives. Ultimately, wholesome sacrifice for wealth entails viewing sacrifices as strategic investments in one's future, balancing expert and private well-being, and navigating challenges with dedication and a clear imaginative and prescient to reap each economic prosperity and holistic fulfilment. Some healthful habits that can help you reap wealth consist of paying your self first with the aid of directing section of each and every pay check to financial savings or investments, understanding the balance in your bills to control unexpected costs, prioritizing fee discount and disturbing value for your money, depositing raises and bonuses into savings or investments, taking advantage of tax savings thru investments like 401(k) contributions, growing multiple streams of income, saving on daily purchases by searching for discounts, and taking the lengthy view via saving constantly and monitoring development over time. Additionally, conducting an annual economic evaluate to determine emergency savings, investments, insurance, and fees can contribute to long-term wealth building. By adopting these habits and strategies, folks can beautify their monetary well-being, construct wealth sustainably, and work towards attaining their long-term economic goals.

CHAPTER 5

Work Life Balance

Work-life balance has turn out to be more and more precious for professionals, with many prioritizing it over pay and promotions. Research suggests that work-life stability is a quintessential aspect in job satisfaction, influencing career selections significantly. Achieving a stability between work and non-public life can lead to expanded productivity, job satisfaction, and standard well-being. Employers are recognizing the significance of work-life stability in attracting and keeping top talent, with many providing bendy work arrangements to help this balance. Professionals are now seeking roles that furnish both a excessive profits and a balanced workload, such as these in the technological know-how sector, consulting, and executive positions, which offer competitive salaries and flexibility. By prioritizing work-life stability alongside income, persons can create a pleasant career that aligns with their private values and well-being. Strategies to enhance work-life stability while increasing earnings include time blocking to allocate particular time for work and private activities, prioritizing self-care to decrease stress and decorate productivity, learning to say no to pointless commitments, the usage of technology accurately to set boundaries and manipulate time effectively, and discovering a supportive community for encouragement and assistance. Additionally, it's imperative to work more efficiently, delegate tasks, set targets and desires strategically, focus on productiveness instead than busyness, and prioritize physical and intellectual well-being to preserve a healthful work-life balance as an entrepreneur. By enforcing these strategies, humans can gain a harmonious equilibrium between work and non-public life, leading to elevated job satisfaction, productivity, and universal well-being while also working in the direction of bettering their income. To expand productiveness whilst retaining work-life balance, individuals can implement strategies like structuring their day for extended productivity, setting boundaries between work and non-public life, prioritizing self-care, and using productiveness hacks like the Poroporo method to work in focused bursts. By growing a practical agenda that approves for each work and personal activities, folks can acquire a higher balance over time as a substitute than aiming for perfection each day. It's critical to centre of attention on efficiency, delegate tasks, set clear goals, and prioritize bodily and intellectual well-being to preserve a healthful work-life stability as an entrepreneur. Additionally, taking breaks, communicating desires clearly, and looking for support from employers for flexible working preparations can make a contribution to more desirable productivity and common well-being whilst maintaining a harmonious work-life balance. To manipulate time efficaciously for expanded productiveness and work-life balance, folks can enforce a range of techniques outlined in the supplied sources. These techniques include:

- Start each day with a plan: Create a list of tasks, allocate time for each, and organize your day to ensure productivity.

- Minimize distractions: Identify and avoid distractions like social media notifications to hold centre of attention and productivity.

- Delegate tasks: Delegate tasks to team participants to focal point on more necessary responsibilities and increase morale.

- Take breaks: Regular breaks throughout the day help forestall mental exhaustion and preserve productivity.

- Avoid excessive overtime: Excessive extra time can also indicate negative time management; leave work on time to keep a healthful work-life balance.

By incorporating these time administration techniques into daily routines, humans can decorate productivity, minimize stress, and attain a higher work-life balance.

Techniques To Putting Boundaries

Some strategies for placing boundaries encompass the following:

- Reflect on the motives for your boundaries: Understand why boundaries are essential to you and how they benefit your emotional well-being.

- Start with a few boundaries: Introduce boundaries regularly to keep away from feeling overwhelmed and allow time for reflection.

- Consider putting boundaries early on: Establish boundaries and expectations from the beginning to prevent confusion and frustration.

- Be constant with your boundaries: Maintain consistency to give a boost to your original thresholds and beliefs.

- Carve out time for yourself: Allocate on my own time commonly to recharge and keep private well-being.

Don't be afraid to encompass greater boundaries: Consider additional boundaries past what is already in location to in addition help your well-being.

To speak your boundaries successfully to others, it is quintessential to comply with these key steps:

- Start small: Begin by way of putting boundaries progressively to enable for adjustment and grasp from others.

- Prepare for pushback: Anticipate that others may additionally withstand your boundaries initially, especially if they have been unaware of them before. Be affected person and understanding as they adapt to the new expectations.

- Be regular and compassionate: Maintain consistency in reminding others about your boundaries and observe through with any imperative actions whilst demonstrating kindness and consideration for their feelings.

By imposing these strategies, humans can speak their boundaries truely and assertively, fostering healthier relationships and making sure that their wants and limits are respected.

Actions To Take

To enlarge income, individuals can take a variety of movements as outlined in the supplied sources:

- Ask for a Pay Increase: Request a elevate from your present day corporation by way of showcasing your cost and contributions to the company.

- Look for a Better-Paying Job: Explore job opportunities that offer higher salaries and higher benefits to amplify your income.

- Start a Side Gig: Engage in part-time work or freelancing to supplement your earnings and discover new opportunities.

- Turn Your Hobby Into A Business: Monetize your abilities and passions by means of beginning a business associated to your hobbies or interests.

- Teach What You Know: Share your know-how through blogging, freelance writing, public speaking, or teaching to generate extra income.

- Rent Out a Room: Consider renting out a room in your domestic for more income, both on a non permanent or long-term basis.

- Go Back to School: Invest in schooling or certifications to beautify your skills and qualifications, leading to better-paying job opportunities.

- Get a Second Job: Take on a part-time job with bendy hours to supplement your essential profits source

Recommendations

Recommendations to Increase Your Income

1. Develop Marketable Skills: Invest in gaining knowledge of new competencies or enhancing present ones that are in demand in your industry. This can make you extra valuable to employers or clients,

leading to manageable salary increases or higher rates for your services.

2. Pursue Career Advancement Opportunities: Seek out opportunities for promotions, raises, or higher-paying positions inside your present day corporation or in the job market. Networking, showcasing your achievements, and taking on additional obligations can assist you pass up the career ladder.

3. Start a Side Business or Freelancing: Consider beginning a facet business or freelancing in your spare time to generate additional income. This can be a way to

monetize your hobbies, expertise, or passion projects.

4. Invest in Real Estate or Stocks:

Explore funding opportunities in real estate, stocks, or different assets that have the workable to generate passive income. Be sure to lookup and understand the risks and rewards associated with each funding option.

5. Negotiate Your Salary or Rates:

Don't be afraid to negotiate your earnings or rates when starting a new job, asking for a raise, or discussing contracts with clients. Research industry standards and be prepared to make a sturdy case for why you deserve more.

6. Take on Additional Work or Projects: Consider taking on more work or projects to extend your income. This should involve working overtime, taking on freelance gigs, or finding part-time opportunities that align with your capabilities and interests.

7. Educate Yourself on Personal Finance: Learn about private finance, budgeting, and investing to make informed choices about managing your money effectively. Understanding how to save, invest, and make clever economic choices can assist you grow your wealth over time.

8. Explore Passive Income Streams: Look for approaches to generate passive income, such as creating and selling

digital products, investing in dividend-paying stocks, or renting out property. Passive income streams can furnish a regular supply of revenue with minimal ongoing effort.

9. Seek Professional Development Opportunities: Attend workshops, seminars, or courses to beautify your expert abilities and knowledge. Continuous getting to know can open up new possibilities for career growth and earnings advancement.

10. Set Clear Financial Goals: Define your monetary desires and create a sketch to reap them. Whether it's saving for a

predominant purchase, constructing an emergency fund, or growing your typical income, having clear objectives can help you remain encouraged and targeted on your financial success.

www.ingramcontent.com/pod-product-compliance
Lightning Source LLC
Chambersburg PA
CBHW071049290526
45795CB00004B/1404